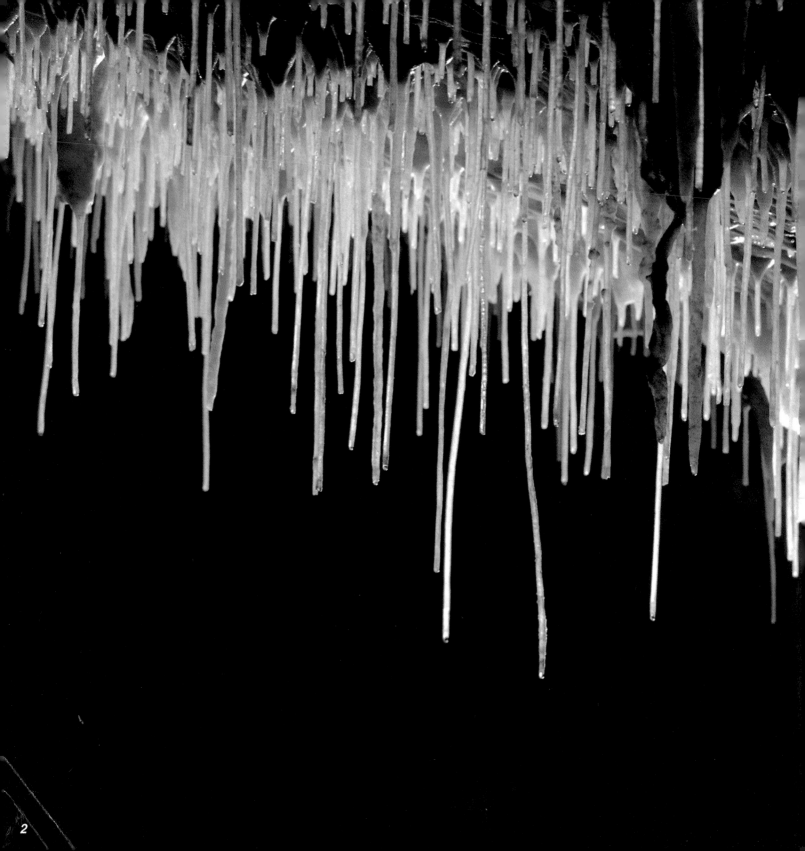

Published by	**Postojna jama, tourism,** Postojna, Slovenia. For the publisher: **Matjaž Berčon**
Editorial board:	**Jerko Čehovin, Miran Fajdiga,** president, **Dr Peter Habič, Miran Lapanja, Ferdo Podboj, Srečko Šajn**
Text:	**Dr Matjaž Kmecl**
Translation from Slovene:	**Anne Čeh**
Language editors:	**Paul O'Mahony, Hugh Brown, Paul Townend**
Editors:	**Dr Peter Habič, Srečko Šajn, Sabina Paternost**
Photographs:	**Franc Golob** 1, 2, 4, 5, 6, 10, 11, 12, 14, 15, 23, 26, 30, 31, 34, 35, 36, 37, 38, 39, 40, 41, 42, 46, 49, 50, 57, 73, 80 ,90, 94, 101, 102, 104, 105, 106, 108, 109, 110,111,112,113,114,115, 116, 117, 118, 119, 120, 121, 122, 123, 124, 125, 126, 127, 128, 129, 130, 131, 132, 133, 134, 135, 136, 137, cover pages 1 and 4
	Dr France Habe 7, 13, 18, 20, 22 ,24, 28, 45, 51, 58, 61, 66, 67, 68, 69, 71, 72, 74, 75, 76, 77, 85, 88, 92, 93, 100, 107, 138, 139
	Dr Peter Habič 16, 43, 62, 97
	Dr France Habe, Benjamin Šmid 19
	Oldrich Kadrnka, Zrinka Šilhard-Kadrnka 3, 21, 32, 63, 64, 65, 70, 79, 89, 140
	Valika Kuštor 81, 82, 83, 84, 86
	Konrad Lampe 53, 54, 98
	Egon Kaše 8, 9, 33
	Emil Maraž 52, 87
	Ivan Mikec-Mitja 47, 55, 56, 59, 60, 95, 96, 99
	Peter Skoberne 44, 48, 78, 91, 103
	Notranjski muzej 25, 27, 29
The map of the Cave – after the charts of the Institute of Karst Research, ZRC SAZU, drawn by:	**Franc Golob**
Lay-out:	**Srečko Šajn**
Photolithographs	**Grafika,** Ilirska Bistrica, **ČukGraf,** Postojna
Printing:	**ČukGraf,** Postojna, 2006 VIII edition

This book has been published in Croat, English, German, French, Italian, Slovene and Spanish.

CIP - Kataložni zapis o publikaciji
Narodna in univerzitetna knjižnica, Ljubljana

551.44(497.4 Postojna)
779:551.44(497.4 Postojna)

KMECL, Matjaž
    Postojna Caves : enter travaller, into this immensity! / Matjaž Kmecl ; [translation from Slovene Anne Čeh ; photographs Franc Golob ... [et al.] ; the map of the Cave - after the charts of theInstitute of Carst Resech, ZRC SAZU, drawn by Franc Golob]. - 8th ed. - Postojna : Postojnska jama, Tourism, 2006

Prevod dela: Postojnska jama

ISBN 86-81687-03-4
227084032

Cover pages 2 and 3: Visitors who signed the "Golden Autograph Book" during the first half of the 19th century included statesmen, artists, scientists, explorers...

1, 2 Millennia within the enduring and sombre attraction between water and stone give birth to fragile white lace dreamily suspended from dark subterranean ceilings. Mother Nature has used her imagination to the full in the Postojna Caves. Whilst the cavernous spaces take one's breath away, theattractive tiny gems, the moments of poetry, gladden the heart.
The start of a stalactite. A drop of water searches for a way through a stony subterranean fissure until it hangs above the empty space. The following drop of water forces it to drop, but before its does a miniscule amount of dissolved limestone will be deposited here. If the drops are tiny, these slim, fragile tubes are created. Whenever there is a greater volume of water, a column comes into being, often consisting of tens of cubic metres of pearly sinter.

Matjaž Kmecl

Postojna Caves

Enter traveller, into this immensity!

Postojna, 2006

Immensum ad antrum aditus.
Enter traveller, into this immensity!

8

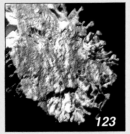

A unique and strangely attractive landscape with blossoming gardens

44

Europe's enthusiasm for witch-hunting was even fiercer here. Unusual tales abound, including that of the knight Erasmus

56

How the Postojna Caves were gradually revealed

82

How Postojna's pride in possessing a site of world interest evolved in practical terms

92

An intermingling of nature and culture in Postojna's marvel

100

3   A. Schaffenrath, *Ansichten der Adelsberger und Kronprinz Ferdinands – Grotte* (The Postojna Caves), 1830

Immensum ad antrum aditus.

Enter traveller, into this immensity!

"Enter traveller, into this immensity!" the ancients would have said, opening wide the gate into the Postojna underworld. Despite its size, the cave beyond is neither the largest in the world nor utterly immense, and certainly not the only one, but it is probably the most famous and the most beautiful. "Immensum ad antrum aditus" is written above the main entrance. Many more entrances exist, both known and unknown, visible, less visible and totally invisible – for water, air and man – but man has been entering through this one for a thousand years, and for the last two hundred of them in vast numbers.

5

3-6 The pictures on these two pages might be entitled: Four Ways into The Caves, in the past (far left), as painted over 200 years ago by Schaffenrath, the surroundings were bare, the bridge over the sinkhole distant, with an idyllic scene of a shepherd with his flock and a marvelling townsman. Today's picture depicts the Caves' Restaurant and starting point for tours. On return, the visitor must pass on foot through the standard exit, soon to discern in the white, shining sinter-decorated ceiling and walls a gateway into Postojna's beauty.

4

6

7   *Water Lily (Nymphaea alba)*

10

7-10 Inside, in the dark, rocky heart, metronomic dripping can be heard falling onto stone. But time passes slowly here and there is minimal change throughout the years. Outside, water-lilies in some pond or lake flower over and over, to vanish again. Blossoming below, the great, snow-white BRILLIANT, so lovely it was chosen as the Caves' symbol, has remained undimmed by time and heedless of night or day, the seasons, years or centuries. Nor do its surroundings alter. Only when the rain outside persists does the dripping become livelier, the caves wetter.

9

13   *Predjama*

11-13 A somewhat Bohemian muddle of curtains and roots, macaroni tubes and pillars, timelessness and creation, long slim stalactites and stalagmites so wide they hardly fit one's preconceptions of such formations.

14, 15 Incredible sinter forms follow one after the other – be they softly idyllic or sharp-toothed FOSSILISED MONSTERS.

16, 17   Postojna

18   The Pivka Basin

16-18 It is here at Postojna that the world begins to open up towards the sea – with the broad, easily viewed Pivka Basin itself a memorial to hundreds of thousand of years of activity by earthly forces demolishing, shifting and continuously accumulating. Hidden far below the surface here is the watershed between the Adriatic and the Black Sea, and the waters from there pour in one or the other direction. With around 8,000 inhabitants, Postojna is situated on an ancient route into the interior known as the Postojna Gap. Centuries ago, the area was already a developed administrative and trade centre for a wider region. A new era of interest in its unusual and almost unique subterranean world led to the further development of Postojna. The town's hotel service has been world renowned since the last century.

19 Some 1,000 beds are available to travellers in Postojna. Located immediately in front of the entrance to the Caves, the large hotel complex is surrounded by beautiful forests, with an equally lovely panorama across the Pivka Basin and the nearest mountain chain.

A brief, telegraphic kind of description will suffice for those pressed by haste, impatience and restlessness:

Postojna Caves have been forming throughout the last two million years. Above them, Mediterranean air meets with that of the mainland, producing copious rainfall (up to 1600 litres per m^2 annually). All of this water then percolates through the fractured limestone strata, its ceaseless dripping creating in the hollows of the interior something Henry Moore called Nature's most wonderful gallery, – or words to that effect – a stony, crystalline fairyland: forests of stalactites and stalagmites; gigantic, frequently baroque-like chiselled columns; countless unusual figures; translucent stony draperies; exquisite porcelain pans holding water. The largest stalagmite, known as The Giant, stands some 16m high, layered and poured over with 1,400 m^2 of sinter. The most beautiful, called the Brilliant – now the symbol of the Postojna Caves – can, with its symmetrical, upward-streaming loveliness, compete with the finest Gothic cathedral pillars and with its translucent, pure colour and smoothness, with the body of the softest female beauty. One of the subterranean spaces contains a 45 metre-high underground mountain; the so-called Concert Hall, some 40 metres high, can hold up to 10,000 visitors at once. Here is a working post office, here numerous concerts and dances have been held, here musicians such as Pietro Mascagni have performed. The Hall's exceptional acoustics produce echoes so strong and so frequent that radiophonic recording has proved very difficult or even impossible. Should there be more rain "above", the concert audience may share in a little more of that tens-of-thousands-of-years dripping that has created all the visible and invisible marvels of the Postojna Caves; for all these scarcely imaginable stony creations came into existence through the perpetual dripping of limestone-laden water upon the same spots, some of the calcite being deposited as the water strikes the ground and before it drains away. Elsewhere, this calcite accumulates from slowly drifting waters, like wax from a burning candle. If the water comes from long fissures in the earth or from overhanging rockfaces, lovely stone draperies as, light and fragile as the world-famous lace from nearby Idrija, are formed. It was these wonders that led the famous Italian speleologist, Pietro Parenzan, from Taranto, to paraphrase the ancient Latin words "gutta cavat lapidem" into "gutta aedificat lapidem": not only does the drop hollow out the stone, it also creates it. And what stone! Not all at once, but with its ceaseless dripping: "non vi, sed saepe cadendo".

Postojna's entire cave system extends over some 23 km. From the initial few hundred metres accessible 200 years ago, the modern visitor takes a route along 5.2 km of prepared and maintained paths with another kilometre or so through an entrance from another side. All this has been maintained in an exemplary manner: marvellously illuminated by electricity since 1884; small electric trains, each taking 120 visitors; guides speaking nine languages; easy, well-fenced walkways and paths; bridges; railings, where required, and so on. In 1872, when the first tracks were laid into the cave, the guides themselves pushed their customers along in two-seater carriages. The beginning of this

18

20   *Zalog, Postojna*

century saw the introduction of petrol engines, to be replaced by electric trains after the Second World War. During the summer season, when northern and central Europeans wend their way to the Adriatic, the greater part of them take the route through the "Postojna Gap", the lowest lying point through the Alpine-Dinaric ranges. At this time, the trains through Postojna Caves run every half-hour, and even out of "high" season they run at least once an hour. Not to make it too easy, part of the tour must be done on foot – and, for a moment, the lights are extinguished to complete the impression of underworld secrecy and man's sense of being lost. The darkness is truly extreme, as is the deafening water rushing on all sides near and far, and the echoing drips. Were it not for the visiting group being even louder, perhaps on account of their sudden fear, the sense of abandonment at the heart of these natural blind forces would be final and complete.

21, 22 *The Modrijan Mill, Postojna*

20-22 In succession outside: spring, summer, autumn and winter, rainy and sunny days, heat and cold, flowers wither, the leaves colour. Time passes rapidly, engulfing man and his work – everything, including this old mill which must be restored from time to time.

23 The Modrijan Mill, Postojna

23, 24 A relic of the past worthy of attention stands in the vicinity of this large hotel, next to a modern car park. On the river that vanishes under ground, a former owner set up a mighty mill, now renovated. Exhibitions and similar events are held here. The lower section of the mill still floods when heavy rain prohibits the river from flowing underground all at once ... the fate of all water mills.

Archaeologists often excavate around caves, and the remains of a cave civilisation have also been found at the entrance to Postojna. Close by is the famous Predjama Castle – an almost inaccessible mediaeval castle fortification at the mouth of a great subterranean tunnel with high walls. In a section of the "old" Postojna Caves, the Gallery of Old Signatures contains one dated 1213, defnitely proven for this period. Other signatures prove that visitors were particularly numerous during the revolutionary periods and Protestantism of the 16th century, amongst them both prince and transgressor. Towards the end of the 17th century, the number of visitors seems to have waned but the first more detailed written descriptions began to make their appearance. In his famous monograph on the main Slovene regions, entitled "The Glory of the Duchy of Carniola" and published in 1689, Janez Vajkard Valvasor reported that the Postojna Caves had long been known. By the start of the 19th century, with the corresponding increase in interest in the natural sciences, the immediate and further surroundings of this place were renowned for their interesting natural features. It is here that the Alpine-Dinaric world meets the Mediterranean; here rules the ancient Slovene deity, Triglav, with his three heads: one to perceive the heavens, one to gaze at earth, a third to control the underworld. Diverse flora and fauna meet and mingle here, as do the warmth of the Mediterranean south and the cold winds of the north. The ground opens up in great chasms, intermittent lakes appear and disappear twice a year, rivers flow from beneath hills to lose themselves again in others, vast forests and wild mountains stretch between. The most prolific of meadows border on bare stone without any real transition; all is brimful of life of every kind.

It was customary in the Europe of two hundred years ago for feudal nobility to take an interest in nature. There is, for instance, a memorial near Ljubljana, some thirty to forty kilometres from Postojna, standing at the foot of pleasant St Lovrenc Hill that commemorates a past visit by the King of Saxony. He made a special journey down here in order to view a then unknown flower – Daphnae blagayana, a species of mezereon. The king continued his journey to include the Postojna Caves with its flowers of stone. But, before him, the long road from Vienna had been risked by the Habsburg Emperor Franz I. It was while lights were being set throughout the caves in his honour, in 1818, that a local man, Luka Čeč, discovered the continuation of the cave. Returning in great elation from beyond a huge dividing wall, he announced, "There's a new world here, a new Paradise!" And so Ferdinand, the Habsburg heir, was able to visit the Postojna Caves the following year along new, more exciting routes. The Congress Hall, named as such to commemorate the Fourth World Speleological Congress held here, in 1824 saw the first of the Whit Monday dances and social gatherings that led in future decades to Whit Monday becoming Postojna Cave Day. After the completion of the Southern Railway from Vienna to Trieste via Ljubljana in 1857, numerous special trains came to Postojna in celebration. The first mass wave of visitors from near and far had begun. Nevertheless, everyone who wished to enter still had to call at the local grocery and register the number of visitors, order the guide and lighting

25, 26 Since records of visitors began, 24 million people have viewed the Postojna caves. For some 170 years, they have been considered some of the most beautiful, largest and most accessible caves in Europe. Old photos show that the sometimes almost unbelievable throngs are not merely a contemporary phenomenon, as the cave trains run without interruption through sections of the 20 km long interior.

27

men. Of course, an entrance fee was also paid – 30 kreutzers for the Cave Fund and 30 for each guide. Visitors signed the visitors' book and, formalities concluded, the long trek through the cave began.

During the first decade, a total of 6,500 visitors was recorded; only half a century later the same number was noted annually and, just before the Second World War, almost as many every month. Today, at the height of the summer season, sometimes double this number gather daily! 900,000 throughout the year! The war in former Yugoslavia has meant that in recent years the number of visitors has again fallen slightly.

In the more than 180 years that have passed since 1818, Postojna Caves have become renowned as one of the world's great sights. One who takes its almost unbelievable paths should pause for a moment to remember that these secret places preserve the memory of two million years of geological history, tens of thousands of years of sinter formations and wonderlands and nearly 25 million human visitors drawn by research, curiosity, "a pioneering spirit", courage and wonder at the world. As we gradually enter the coolness of the caves – a permanent 10° C – from the heat of the summer (or during the winter into their warmth) through icicles that decorate the ceiling at the entrance, we should reflect that although at first glance all this seems quite natural, we are in fact venturing deep into the heart of something that has, throughout centuries and millennia, filled man with fear and humility, legends and horrific imagination. Of course, those who wish to enter the cave as a routine, as a payable tourist rite, may take it as such. Life demonstrates that every moment can be the first. The ancient Greeks were convinced that one cannot step into the same river twice because everything flows on, everything is continually altering – our lives, in particular. The same is valid when visiting Postojna's subterranean miracles: on each occasion time resounds differently within, the ardent enthusiasm of Luka Čeč as he discovered the extension of "Paradise" in the past can be sensed anew, it is always possible, at least in one's thoughts and feelings, as Nietzsche would have it, to fling a burning truss of straw down into the biblical darkness, trembling before the unknown, dangerous, fathomless beyond. Or, again, to always smile gently at the benevolent picture of all those visiting, countless lovers united by the darkness, who have, in this subterranean border between wonderland and fear, light and dark, pressed each other's hands in mutual inclination: for them, this is a subterranean Venice. And again calling to mind all those questions to which man has never found the answers.

This should suffice as a short summary for the hasty tourist who wants to see, but not too much, to enjoy for a moment rather than ponder; for the world is wide, and there is much to be seen. Yet no one should wish to pass this by.

28

27, 28 Lively events are always taking place close to the entrance into the immense cave. But even without the atmosphere, here we have anticipation, excitement and a somewhat festive air, as before some great experience.

29

29, 30 In the early days, travellers with money were able to arrange to be carried into the caves rather than tackle the dark and dangerous world below on foot. By 1872, two-seater carriages on rails were being pushed through the caves. The modern tourist cannot enter without the small electric trains busily running in and out. Only deep in the heart of the caves does one leave the train and walk.

31, 32 As shown on the following pages, the train tracks sometimes divide to avoid some great column. Subtle care is always taken of the preservation and simultaneous revelation that is beautiful.

33 The GREAT MOUNTAIN, also known as CALVARY, in one of the greatest monuments in the Postojna Caves. At the junction of three galleries the ceiling of a gigantic gallery collapsed, creating a 45-m high hill nowadays overgrown with sinter formations. The ride by train ends below this and visitors gather around guides speaking diverse languages, starting off from here for a closer inspection of the Caves and their wonders.

30

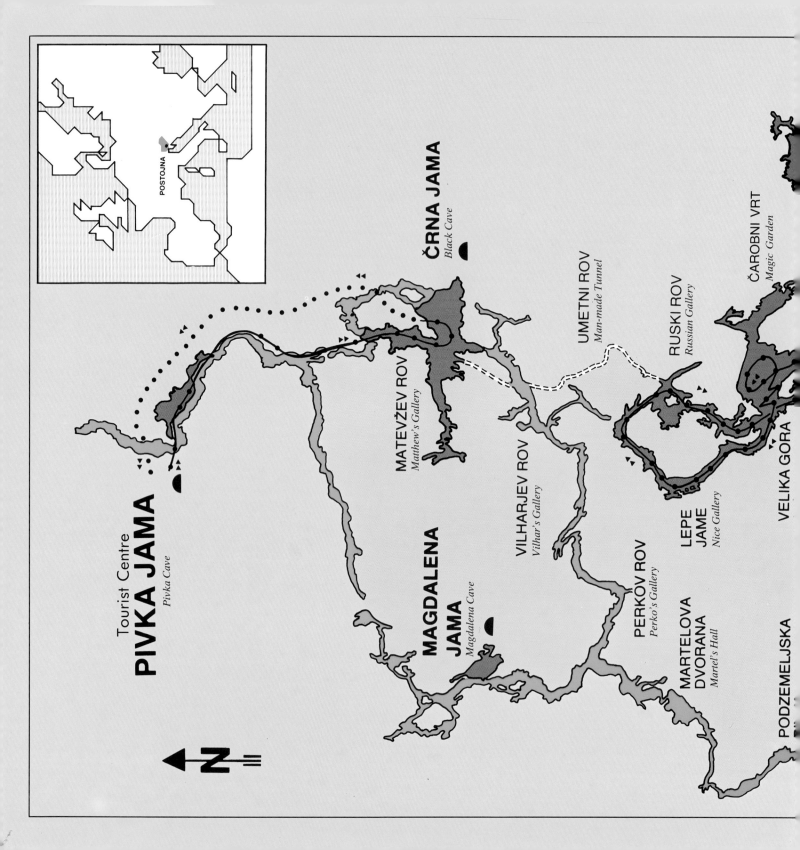

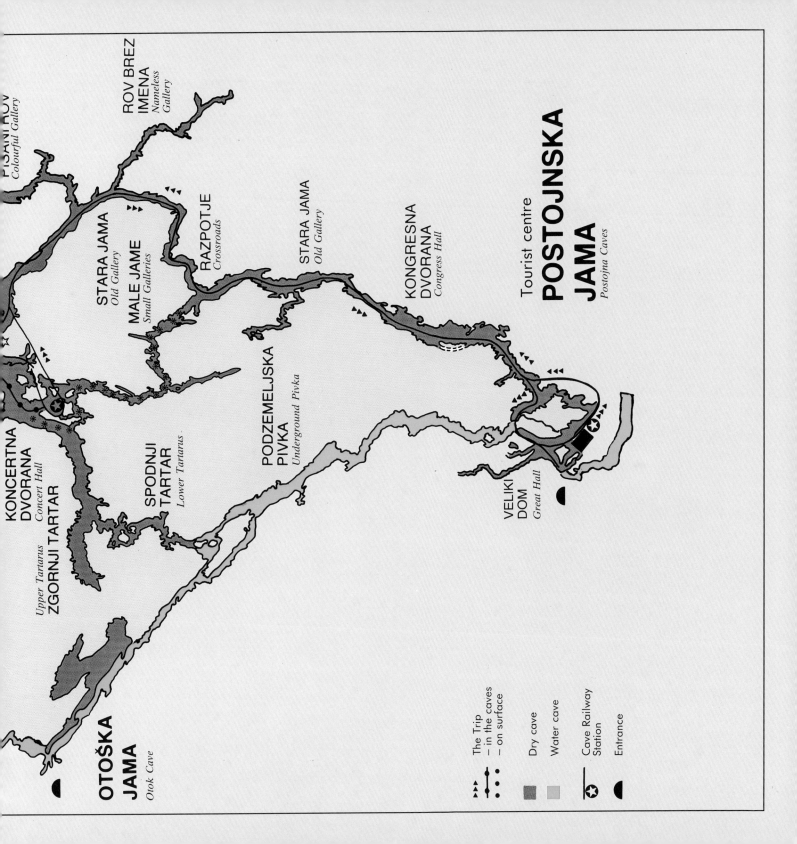

PISANI ROV
Colourful Gallery

ROV BREZ
IMENA
*Nameless
Gallery*

STARA JAMA
Old Gallery

MALE JAME
Small Galleries

RAZPOTJE
Crossroads

STARA JAMA
Old Gallery

KONCERTNA
DVORANA
Concert Hall
ZGORNJI TARTAR
Upper Tartarus

SPODNJI
TARTAR
Lower Tartarus

PODZEMELJSKA
PIVKA
Underground Pivka

KONGRESNA
DVORANA
Congress Hall

Tourist centre
**POSTOJNSKA
JAMA**
Postojna Caves

VELIKI
DOM
Great Hall

OTOŠKA
JAMA
Otok Cave

The Trip
– in the caves
– on surface

Dry cave

Water cave

Cave Railway
Station

Entrance

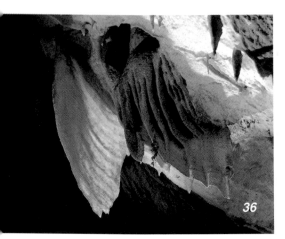

36, 37 Hanging side by side are the LIGHT and DARK CURTAINS. The path from beneath the GREAT MOUNTAIN leads into the BEAUTIFUL CAVE over the RUSSIAN BRIDGE that was constructed by Russian prisoners-of-war during the First World War.

34, 35 The picture shows the TENT, and behind it, the unusual, baroque COLUMNS in the BEAUTIFUL GALLERIES. Though the eye may search, it will not find one centimetre of space here without some kind of decoration, limestone glaze or frosted covering. Visitors seem astonished and slightly at a loss.

38 The train ride ends beneath the GREAT MOUNTAIN. A quietness descends, hushed by this enormous cave, visitors gather around their guides. Everything has been arranged so that it is impossible to lose the way – which would be inadvisable to say the least.

39

39-41 There's a crystal pan full of water at every step and a variegated alley of pillars such as, for example, at the CROSSROADS.

40

42 A little further and the stacks and columns are so close there is barely space for a path between them.

43-45 Outside, at first glance it might appear that nothing is concealed beneath the surface. Here, we see the motorway running from Ljubljana towards the sea, the extensive forests and meadows, the typical Karst poljes where water collects from autumn to spring. Nevertheless, here above, much may be sensed that indicates the vulnerability of this world and the special link between the interior and the surface. A sudden chasm, a deeply incised fissure in the stone. In between, the innumerable varieties and colours of flowers that include some half dozen species of Daphne.

44   *Mezereon (Daphnae)*

A unique and strangely attractive landscape with blossoming gardens

46 Amidst the stony fantasies are a series of PANS WITH PEARLS.

The traveller with more time at his/her disposal should take a look at the surrounding countryside. All the better if this can be more often, during the different seasons of the year; the area has so many unique and strange attractions. Great bare expanses of grass interchange with impenetrable, dark, cold forests; deep within them wolves can still be found, and hundreds of bears have been sighted by hunters. But do not worry: they do not harass travellers,

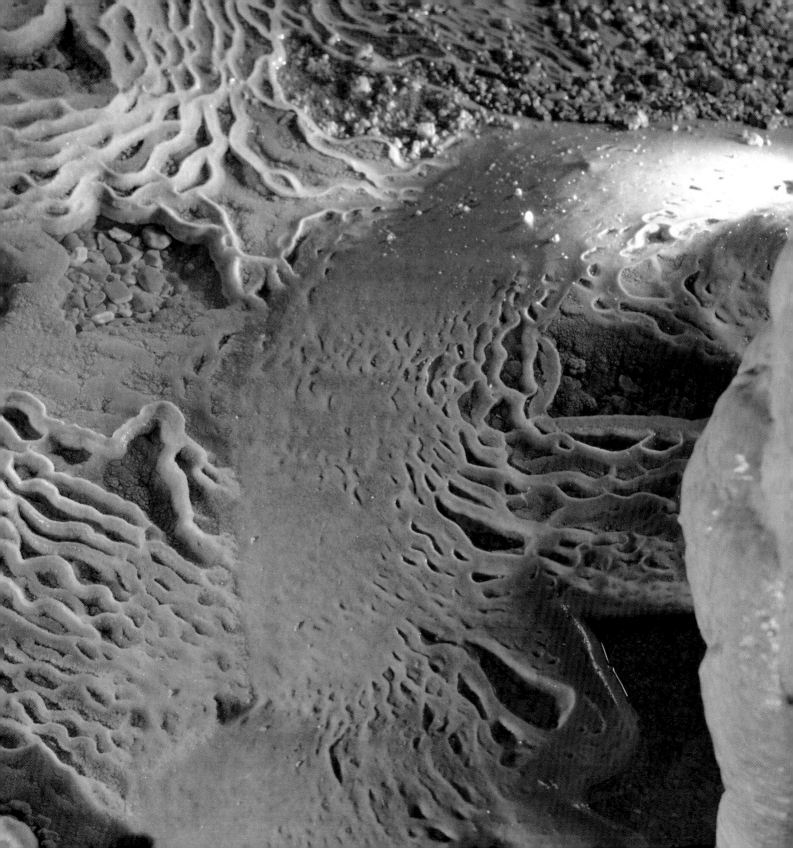

47 Peacock butterfly (Vanessa io)

47-49 With his innate claustrophobic fear of darkness, man's thoughts turn towards the outside, where perhaps the peonies bloom in isolated meadows or rare groves (Paeonia officinalis; mascula). Abundant where the hand of man refrains, whole gardens of these native flowers can sometimes be found. Butterflies (Inachis), rest upon them. In its own way, the underground blooms here too. Beneath the ceiling gigantic flowers and tall, ancient trees spout from the floor in grey and black stone.

48 Peony (Paeonia officinalis)

let alone attack them! Growing in the spring meadows is a wealth of flowers that only a central European would normally expect to find in a garden. Particularly noticeable are the peony (Paeonia); the ordinary (P. officinalis) and the great-leaved (P. mascula) varieties. Entire sunny glades or meadow borders blush here and there with their large, cardinal red single blooms full of golden stamens. Irises of every kind – ilyrica, pallida, sambucina, graminea, sometimes whole colonies – to the top of slopes and hills, true flower beds and plantations by Mother Nature, often together with peonies. Towards summer various gladioli, the tall great yellow gentian (Gentiana lutea), beautiful lilies – the orange (bulbiferum), the Carnic lily (Lilium arniolicum) of rather unpleasant odour, so unbecoming in a lily, the martagon lily (Lilium martagon). By the start of April the lovely Carniolan cowslip (Primula carniolica) can be found in damp spots – truly endemic in these regions; varieties of daphne grow over the light sunny rocks, in fact all six known to botanists in this part of nature's world. The highest peaks are a true parade of alpine blooms mingled with those of the Dinaric Karst. Hairy edraianthus with sub-alpine white narcissi mix with thistles (Cirsium), jurinea and knapweed (Centaurea). In between the tall spires of mulleins (Verbascum), every species of wormwood (Artmesia) whilst high above, the globeflower (Trollius), springside or follow each other through the seasons. Probably every European nation has a legend of how one day, when God was creating the world, setting this and that in clearings here and there, his bag of flowers burst, emptying out its contents in a single heap. Probably every nation has reason enough to narrate this tale – if nothing else from a love of their native land. But the bag of flowers belonging to that Creator certainly emptied out here, including about ten varieties of plant indigenous only here, growing nowhere else. And if we consider the world below the surface, the unique, unrepeatable blooms are even more – the transitory and the perpetual, the living and the stone. He who desires at least some preparation for the beauties of the Postojna underworld should first walk above it – somewhere between March and July.

In summertime, the grassy plateaus brown over, scorched. The water leaves the surface for the interior, the ground rapidly filtering it away. The entire landscape glows, however, in the vivid, gloriously full colours of autumn. The dry limestone renders beeches even more golden, maples an even sunnier yellow. Hawthorn (Craetagus), buckthorn (Rhmanus) and all the other bushes add numerous other nuances of colour and, on the slightly warmer, sunny slopes streams of bright red Cotinus pour over the ground, its aggressive beauty uncaptured by any painter's imagination or any poet's pen. "Ground glowing in darks rays of sun" is what Srečko Kosovel (1904-1926), the greatest poet from the Karst world, would say. – The feverish brevity of his life spoke out in a thousand verses – with but a single idea, that of his own secretive, native world, warm and sheltering as a way of life, and the Europe of the future, its murky twentieth century fate. Europe has almost forgotten him, coming as he did from too tiny a world, too impoverished a family, dying too young, though his beauty and the love of his people have remained. Whisperingly, they accompany the traveller through the autumnal Karst and its multicoloured melancholy. Whether

we realise this or not, the wind is relating a verse by this youthful poet, dispersing it between the red-leaved cherries and dark pines:

> I drifted with a golden boat
> Along the red waters of the evening
> Between trees
> And grassy banks.
> I drifted,
> I, the golden sailor ...

The Mediterranean reaches right to the Pivka Basin and Postojna Gap, and it is here that the vast forests indicating the "interior" begin. Three hundred years ago, Valvasor wrote that this "vast" dark, dangerous forest that had mercilessly rejected any extension of the Mediterranean was some 3 leagues or about 23 modern kilometres wide, even at its narrowest point. Within range of Postojna, towards Ljubljana, the traveller came to Ravbarkomanda – the start of a world inhabited by ruffians and outcasts, people not acknowledging either divine or human laws, never having succeeded in accustoming themselves to them. They killed merchants and stole goods and animals – here many a retailer and carrier met their end, for only the law of the strongest, fastest, most cunning and most violent ruled here. Honest and relatively wealthy persons did not dare to traverse this region without a guard; carriers only travelled in groups of several wagons together. The forest was so immense, so dark, so full of caves, collapses, chasms, cliffs and hiding places, so overgrown and uneven that, even after only a few paces into it, it was possible to find cover and hide, to vanish. Count Janez Vajkard Valvasor, otherwise a man of enlightenment, thirsty for knowedge, believed above all that the devil incarnate ruled this forest, pasturing his creeping creatures, the dormice supposed to be his, and all else here. People recounted to him tales of dragons beneath hills letting water out of the earth's openings only twice a day; that there were apparitions in the caves strangely linked to the thunder in the sky. It is true that the ground is surprisingly hollowed out around here, water running from it and into it so strangely that what is observed is frequently at odds with all common experience and knowledge about such things. Almost as if established physical laws are invalid. Nature has created so many unexpected devices, siphons, tunnels, collecting places and so on that, in the end, it is possible to clarify all these extraordinary phenomena, in appearance frequently astonishing, in a reasonable manner. The greatest and most renowned, unusual feature is the disappearing, intermittent lake at Cerknica, more than 20 km^2 in size and known to the ancient Greek geographer Strabo and later described in detail in the 16th century. For half the year, this lake is water, half the year a grassy meadow. Freakish. Countless attempts have been made to force it to be either a permanent lake or a permanent meadow but, despite modern techniques, none have succeeded. The strange interplay of two arch elements continues. From time immemorial it has been possible to fish, hunt, cut hay, or even reap from the same place.

50, 51 Here and there numerous stalagmites and stalactites standing upright and hanging down become a stone fairy tale, as baroque pillars in myriads colours or great extinguished candles with caps of stony wax. Snow-white when the dissolved calcium carbonate from which nature creates them is not mixed with other minerals; iron and magnesium in the water render them ochre, red or yellow with an occasional other colour.

52   Mt Snežnik

52 Affectionately known to its inhabitants as "the sunny side of the Alps", Slovenia is a land more than half covered by forest. Here, in the surroundings of Postojna Caves, the forest is at its most extensive. To the people of the coast, it was always a dark wall separating the sunny Mediterranean from the cold, shady interior. And because the underworld additionally produced extraordinary and fearful signs, everything here seemed dangerous or uncertain.

53

53   *Edible dormouse (Glis glis)*

54   *Brown bear (Ursus arctos)*

53, 54 Numerous dormice, small rodents that used to be thought of as the Devil's creatures, sometimes still hunted today, creep into beech trees. Hunters also carefully tally some 300 bears – large, mostly timid creatures that usually turn and run when chanced upon. An encounter is quite an experience!

54

An attempt is being made to produce a series of reservoirs and power stations along a sequence of stepped Karst poljes between Postojna and Ljubljana. Between them, underground, runs a single river with various names (the Pivka, the Unica, the Ljubljanica) but the phenomenon is too interesting, too exceptional, meeting with too much opposition from the Greens and there are also questions as to whether the scheme would succeed.

55   *Capercaillie (Tetrao urogallus)*

56   *Red deer (Cervus elaphus)*

55, 56 An arrogant capercaillie and mighty red deer – flesh and blood, not stone.

Europe's enthusiasm for witch-hunting was even fiercer here. Unusual tales abound, including that of the knight Erasmus.

Thus, it is hardly strange that people here are rather circumspect – at every step the ground teaches them that appearances should not be trusted, that the devil may be hiding behind every bush. When all Europe was hunting witches, this was carried on here with double fervour. A late 17th century chronicle states that "the country thereabouts is well-stocked" with witches because it is "very savage and toads and other poisonous grubs creep about in the holes". On Slivnica, a thousand-metre mountain near Cerknica, these creatures gather, dance, hold seances and create storms, which they send out over people from the mountain crevasses. From afar they look like tiny lights. "So that there," wrote the chronicler, "they often make fires, burning many of them, so that more … are burnt at the stake in a single year than have been brought to the stake in the country as a whole since time immemorial, there to be burnt to ashes." And it was here, too, that the final one ended in this manner, even upon the threshold of Enlightenment.

57   *The intermittent Cerknica Lake (Cerkniško jezero)*

58   *Cerknica – Watercourse*

57, 58 Along the banks and dry areas of the Cerknica Lake, which has stirred man's curiosity for at least 2000 years, from ancient Greek geographer Strabo onwards. For half the year a lake, for the other half a pleasant meadow of 26 km². Two thirds of the bottom of the lake is watertight, one third completely full of holes and porous, as seen in the picture below. Whenever a great deal of rain falls, it is unable to drain away all at once; insufficient rain does not fill the hollow. The lake fills up in autumn and empties in summer. Interestingly, it is always full of fish. Attempts at "closing" or halting this process in the lake have all failed. Wonderful bird life is found here.

59, 60   *Roe deer (Capreolus capreolus)*

Postojna Caves could not then remain without their own tales. One such story is of the cave dragon devouring animals and young maidens until someone hit upon the idea of filling a calf skin with quicklime and setting it before the cave for the monster to devour in its greed. The resulting burns and thirst made it gulp down the subterranean waters, ultimately to be destroyed by the quicklime. As the dragon was dying, it roared and roared, to be heard in the farthest village and even beyond.

61

59–62 The immense, dense forests in these regions are full of animals. Roe deer, both large and small are common. Wolves, bears, dormice and red deer, lynx and great birds of prey are another matter. What happens to water here is almost unbelievable – whole rivers flow from the hills and into them, from great apertures or from behind a stone or two or a rocky cliff. Geographers are never quite sure whether to class poljes here as fields or lakes. With its own 5 km long cave with the River Unec running through it and the confluence of two rivers, Planinsko polje is underwater for many months and considered to be one of the largest water caves in the world.

61   The Planina Cave
62   Planina polje

The entire world here seems to be suspended between the sky and Hades, or even Tartarus, between reality and fantasy, between appearance and the truth (often secretive). Simultaneously, it unashamedly shows signs of constant alterations, its own kind of life, a self-will. In its geological past, the whole of the Postojna region seems to have been a lake: the traveller can see this for himself before the cave entrance. Here was a ceaseless falling, sliding, building upagain, pouring out, sinking down, flooding, inflowing and outflowing, emptying and filling, hollowing and eroding: a constant dialogue between two of Triglav's heads – the earthly and the subterranean. Man can scarcely comprehend and can only marvel fearfully.

63 Paths above ground run through countryside such as this; here the path leads to Predjama and its castle.

64-66   Predjama

64-66 Picturesque Predjama Castle, visible from afar, is 9 km from Postojna. Not only is it famous for the ancient legend about the robber knight Erasmus, who was besieged here in 1483 and 1484, and finally killed, but also for its architecture. Hung atop a 123 metres high rockface that is a maze of hollowed galleries and tunnels behind, the castle was almost invincible for many centuries – if indeed anyone ever came across it. Tradition holds that the body of the knight Erasmus lies beneath the great time tree next to the 15th century gothic church on the slope. Traditionally, visitors to the famous castle left their signatures on the walls (the earliest verified signature in the Postojna Gallery of Signatures is from 1213). The old signatures are an interesting part of history, but there are many new ones, too, so the effect is one of graffiti.

63

65

A few kilometres on from the entrance to Postojna Caves one of the most picturesque buildings in Slovenia is located. Mentioned in the introduction, the Predjamski grad, or Predjama Castle, literally suspends in the middle of its 123 metres high rocky cliff – four floors, almost arrogantly plain, unconquered and uncompromising. Man dwelt in the cave behind the castle as far back as 12,000 years ago, during the Late Stone Age and Bronze Age. Earlier fortification stood right in the hollow of the cave, the building we see today was finished only at the end of the 16th century, although its mediaeval history is proven from at least 1202 onwards. An ancient testimony to this is a display in the CastleMuseum itself. Not much imagination is required to ascertain that this castle was ideal for any wilful, rebellious knight: hidden, far from the road, safe, almost inaccessible, with a secret rear entrance through an underground tunnel. And, indeed, the tale of one such robber baron, the knight Erasmus has been handed down to us.

66

67

67-70 Predjama

67-70 Situated below the castle, different and surprising from every angle, and whose artefacts bear witness from prehistory to the present day, and to man's transitory nature, are the caves. Here the Lokva stream submerges entirely, to see daylight again only on the other side of Mt Nanos, as a group of picturesque springs in Vipava.

68

69

Erasmus lived at the end of the 15th century – half a millennium ago. Evidently, he felt himself sufficiently powerful to begin dispensing justice in his own right. When he killed a Lord Marshal at the Emperor's court, he fled as fast as possible to his secret, safe eyrie, continuing to rule the immediate and further surroundings from there. What he needed, he took. If there were animals, he would go to the nearest farmer ploughing a field, unyoke his oxen and take them to his castle. In time tradition would have it that he took only from the rich and not the poor, even helping the latter, but this is scarcely probable. Irrespective of this, the Emperor was kept informed of his deeds so that eventually the ruler commanded the governor of Trieste, Ravbar, to bring a proper end to the matter by capturing Erasmus alive or dead. No one from Ravbar's army knew of Erasmus' hideout, but the knight was so arrogant he went in person to challenge his persecutor, shooting beneath his window and inviting him to his own castle, thereby leaving a trail behind him. The enemy tracked him down, placing four cannon beneath the high rock face; approach

71

72

72   Predjama

71-73 The Knight Erasmus possessed his own coat-of-arms (above), next to which is another winter view of the fortress from below. Some local food prepared for festival days: home cured pork, ham, with grapes, walnuts, olives, rye and buckwheat bread. Only the original juniper gin is missing. It is worth the traveller's while to taste all of these, available in all good inns.

could only be made one by one up the steep, narrow steps with the entrance protected by one well-placed militiaman. Because no other method lay open to him, Ravbar laid siege to the castle, in the conviction that he would starve the defenders out. But those under siege had provided themselves with an additional underground tunnel at the rear, sending down on Shrove Tuesday a roasted bullock cut into quarters to the frozen, starved soldiers below. The soldiers devoured the meat but did not desist in their fighting, convinced that this was the final trick of those under siege. When, some weeks later, they were sent down lamb for Easter and then the first cherries and fresh fish, they began to despair, beginning to believe there was a ceaselessly flowering and fruitful paradise in the underground beneath the castle. But, as Philip of Macedonia once said, every fortification can be taken if only a money-laden ass can enter... "No high, strong and invincible castle exists that does not have its servant who will accept money." Through his own benevolence, Erasmus had become

impertinent towards his besiegers, even sending them his notary along with the gifts of food. And it was this man who was bribed. Sir Erasmus was a man of very regular habits and could be found in the same place at the same time every day carrying out "that which even the Turkish Emperor cannot do via some ambassador or Grand Vizier, but only in person". The bribed servant marked this place by hanging out a small flag and the cannon were aimed at this precise spot. When the time came for firing the light went on in the appropriate window. The cannon gunners were not the best; none of the cannon balls hit Erasmus but smashed into the cliff rocks, which broke off, thereby crushing his head and legs. Thus was the rebellion of the summer 1484 suppressed.

The Castle Museum particularly emphasises this tale. On any pleasant sunny day it is worth taking a seat on the terrace of the inn quite close to this historic site, fortifying oneself with a taste of the meats or sausages cured in the violent north wind known as the "burja", full of scents of pines and other resins.

74

74   *Wild Lake (Divje jezero)*

75   *The Rakov Škocjan Park*

74, 75 Wild Lake, near Idrija; not far off is a good example of a syphonic hollow where, in heavy rainfall, water from the great slopes collects along natural subterranean galleries with such force that it bursts forth up to a metre high. To the right is one of the numerous natural bridges (the small natural bridge in Rakov Škocjan), the arched remains of former cave ceilings.

75

76   *Cerknica – Zelše*

77   *The Kriûna Cave*

76, 77 The tiny church of St. Volbenk in Zelše (built in 1680, hosts summer concerts) is architecture typical of this region; modest, decent, clear and considered in line. Beneath it, cavers in Križna cave.

This wind is, on occasion, so strong it has been known to topple heavy lorries on the open road. Add to this a glass of wine from nearby Vipava or the Karst: Barbara, Teran, Vipavec or the famous Vipava "Green" wine and recall some of those ancient times in the imagination. Far below, a whole stream (the Lokva) disappears into the underworld, a dark crowd of pine trees the cliff edge opposite – it all seems like the end of the world, with not a single path beyond. Close by is a lovely Gothic church from Erasmus´ fifteenth century; growing next to it a centuries´ old lime tree under which, as folklore would have it, the former unlucky knight himself is buried. The whole castle is astonishingly bright and dry with wonderful views over the landscape below. The chambers within are full of old objects and works of art, including a marvellous pietà of white stone, the offspring of inspired imagination of five centuries ago. It is fact that you will not be the first: nowadays, some 600,000 visitors arrive here annually, none of them sorry to have made the trip, so extraordinary and unusual is the whole place.

76

The legend of Erasmus has inspired artistic imagination of every kind. Some pictures are exhibited in the Castle itself and those unable to read Slovene must only regret that they cannot enjoy in the original the immensely picturesque novel by Saša Vuga, entitled "Erasmus of Predjama". Not only this tale, but the surroundings as a whole, invite creativity. Wandering around locally one comes across numerous tiny, pleasant churches, at first glance rustic, upon closer inspection featuring the simple nobility of churches of varying eras. Mostly built of hewn stone and more than 300 years old, they are beautifully decorated. Those farmsteads that survived the rigours of war and eras of brigands are above all pleasing to the eye in their modest subjugation to the landscape, the wild winds, harsh winters and everything else from which they must protect all those entrusted therein.

77

78   *Great Yellow Gentian (Gentiana lutea)*

78-80 In summer, the yellow gentian (Gentiana lutea) blooms amongst the stone pavements; the bitter liquid in its roots is used for Gentian liqueur. In the past, great quantities of this plant were dug up for this purpose, resulting in an increase of drinkers and a decrease in plants. Thesedays the plant is protected. Below, between the CONCERT HALL and the SMALL GALLERIES, the wonderful red-brown crystalline CANOPY shines from beneath the roof. Close by are thousands of large and small stalactites that people would break off as quickly as they once picked the gentians had they too not been protected. Through the majority of people would only have done this out of enthusiasm and love of something beautiful, the resulting decrease would be the same.

As has been noted, Slovenia has 15,000 subterranean caves, chasms and similar, deep forests, ranges of hills, sinkholes and rockfaces, and an honest and loyal people – all of which was ideal for the partisan Liberation Struggle during the last war. Because the Postojna Gap, with its railway to Trieste, was an extremely important and strategic location, the small local population of some 7,000 endured occupation by 2,000 armed soldiers during the Second World War. Attempts to induce fear into the rebellious surroundings were made with hangings, burnings and bombardment, but all in vain. The forests returned with as good as they got. One of the most important partisan actions against the occupation of Postojna was the attack and setting on fire of the store of aeroplane fuel kept by the enemy in the Postojna caves. The Nazi command was convinced that no safer place could be found, sealing up the entrance into the underground and posting a heavy guard out front. But, on the 23 April 1944, a group of partisan saboteurs led by those most familiar with the Postojna underground crept through various tunnels to set fire to this fuel store. A vast cloud of black smoke and the smell of fuel gushed from the main entrance; the fuel was to burn for seven days. The "technique" used to light the fuel was simple: as the group retreated, one of them wrapped a stone in his handkerchief, dipped it the fuel, set it alight and threw it towards the liquid pouring out of the previously holed barrels. But the fire spread extremely rapidly, the fumes engulfing the courageous man, so that for some seconds he was unconscious. When he came to, his comrades were no longer there. This man searched for two days and two nights for an exit. Feeling his way along the underground railway tracks, he even had to hide from the German patrols that unknowingly gave him at least an indication of direction until, scorched and almost naked, he eventually found his way out.

Guides draw the modern visitor's attention to this story, no less dramatic than that of Erasmus, indicating the greater part of the cave that has been black and sooty ever since. Soon after the war, in August 1945, one of the former commandoes brought some special guests here – the Slovene government and the Allied Military Commander of the Central Mediterranean Front, Field Marshal Alexander. Only then could he realise for himself what havoc had been wrought the previous year. The guests heard an account of the story, and were "surprised, astonished and enthusiastic".

At least one other tale should be mentioned, amusingly pickwick-like, and of literary historical interest: the tale of the weird and enthusiastic searcher for the cave beetle, Snakshnepskovsky. This heralds the start of contemporary Slovene novel writing. The actual model for this story was a former merchant and amateur naturalist, Ferdinand Schmidt, from what is today Slovenia's capital, Ljubljana. Almost forgetting his own store, he gathered about himself young enthusiasts, "combing" the countryside with them and observing nature in detail. The same Luka Čeč who, in 1818, discovered the route from the entrance of Postojna Caves into the interior found, in 1831, in the deep darkness of the caves a beetle that was eventually brought to the aforementioned merchant.

A detailed description was sent to the newspapers; the tiny creature was a true sensation because the general conviction was that life without greenery, in the cold and total darkness, was impossible. One of the merchant's young followers, possibly the most talented of them, the writer Fran Erjavec, a kind of Slovene Brehm, turned the matter into a joke and wrote a novel based on the tale. So, at the threshold to Postojna Caves, Slovene speleobiology and novel writing began with this story. The beginnings of Slovene speleobiology were also the world beginnings of this branch of science.

81

84

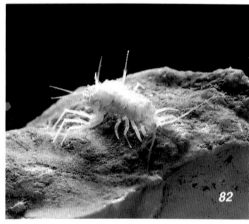

82

83

Later systematic research has revealed over 190 varieties of animal life in the cave darkness, quite a number if we take into consideration that whole animals are tiny, scarcely visible creatures, with some larger ones like leeches, beetles, diptera and even three types of fish. The greatest rarity is the Proteus or "human" fish, which has gradually become the symbol of the Slovene subterranean world and Slovene biology in general. Proteus anguinus is a tailed, amphibian "human" fish up to 30 cm long, and the colour of human skin. Those examples that can be viewed during a tourist trip through the caves are a little darker, as these creatures darken in the light in exactly the same manner as the human body does in sunshine. Breathing through gills as fish do, they also possess atrophied lungs and eyes. They reproduce with eggs but also with living young. Proteus has adapted to underground life by using only an exceptionally small amount of oxygen. Because they do not alter their bodies in growth, as do the majority of amphibians, naturalists have been interested in them for almost two hundred years. Initially, the human fish was considered to be the progeny of the dragon. Three hundred years ago, Valvasor reported very seriously on these rumours and that some farmer had even showed him a captured and killed specimen of such a dragon. After serious and learned biologists such as Laurenti in 1768 had described Proteus, it was a long while before anyone could decide where to classify it in the animal world. The great

85

81   Cave Freshwater Shrimp (Troglocaris anophthalmus)

82   Cave Water Bug (Asellus aquaticus subterroneus)

83   Cave Hopper (Leptodirus Hohenwarti)

84,85   "Human Fish" (Proteus anguinus)

86   Cave Louse (Brachydesmus subterraneus)

81-86 One of the greatest sensations in the exploration of the Postojna underworld was the discovery of living creatures in the eternal darkness. The same Luka Čeč who discovered the entrance into the central caves in 1818 also brought out the first subterranean animal. All these creatures exist without eyes, because they do not require them. The majority of them also do not possess any pigment and are as translucently as the cave sinter. The most famous of them is the "HUMAN" FISH (Proteus anguinus), a salamander or amphibian, a living fossil from the Tertiary Age, that breeds through eggs and live young. Today, this animal is the symbol of Slovenia's caves, as it only dwells in the Dinaric Karst, adapting to other conditions with great difficulty. In earlier times, people considered this strange animal to be some kind of young dragon and even the enlightened Valvasor described it as such. Speleobiology, the study of living cave fauna and flora, began in Postojna.

86

87

87   *Kalec*

88   *Vilenica Cave*

87-90 A few settlements, homesteads, even a castle's remains (Kalec) exist in the open grassy plain above the caves. April sees the Pasque flower (Pulsatilla) nestling here amidst other blooms. Elsewhere in the Slovene Karst, the Vilenica Cave (right), near Sežana, is certainly famous. A meeting of writers from Central Europe gathers here annually. At the entrance to Pivka Jama, a part of the Postojna system, a modern, comfortable camp site well known throughout Europe has evolved.

Linnaeus was convinced it was nothing other than one of the development stages of some lizard, an opinion that prevailed until the start of the 19th century, such was Linneaus' authority. The "human" fish was researched in detail anew and a final confirmation given that this was a distinct species of animal. Because it really is a great anomaly and resident only in the Slovene and Dinaric Karst, it was for a time fashionable to steal these little animals and

89

90

attempt to establish them in other caves in the world – without any great
success, because Proteus is extremely sensitive to its environment. These
hefts in their own way are also part of history, and a return to the start of
speleology and speleobiology, to the cradle of our own origins and existence –
and to the Slovene Karst, whose greatest jewel is the Postojna Caves.

91

91   *Iris (Iris)*

92, 93   *The Škocjan Caves*

91-94 Above ground, an iris (Iris; Illyrian, Siberian, Flag, Grassy-leaved) and, below ground, another exceptional natural wonder – the Škocjan Cave with its fearfully deep subterranean canyon and river and equally wonderful cascade of pans and gigantic hollowed hall. In the autumn, Cotinus colours this dry, drained, sunny, stony and yet overgrown region with such a surprising red that words or pictures to describe it are hard to find.

92

93

94

95

96

95   Alpine Strawberry (Fraggaria vesca)

96   Edible snail (Helix pamatia)

97   Pečinka Cave

95-97 The vegetable, animal and mineral worlds – strawberries, snails and sinter – similar forms, harmonious as one and the same.

Though incredible chasms 1,000 metres deep are to be found in the interior of the Julian Alps, and a seemingly innocent small lake that belches forth huge quantities of water collected from the hills around to percolate through siphons to the lake bottom creates an effect rather like some large artesian well; though the Škocjan Caves are monumental with their vast halls, and 90 metre deep river canyon far beneath the earth's surface; and though they have been entered into the UNESCO World Natural Heritage Register, the Postojna Caves remain a kind of sovereign of world caving. The Postojna and Škocjan Caves, some thirty kilometres apart in the Slovene Karst, offer the visitor two completely different experiences.

98

98   Red squirrel (Sciurus vulgaris)

99   Pond duck (Anas platyrhynchos)

98, 99 Squirrels observe from the trees the traveller in the wild. A flight of wild duck rise from the half-overgrown fish ponds and springtime lakes of the Karst.

Whilst the Škocjan caves are gothically gloomy, with verticals that ceaselessly emphasise the minuteness, frailty and transitory nature of man, the Postojna Caves are somehow affectionate, baroque in their ostentatiousness, embellished at very step with a diversity of details, tunnels, galleries and small caves. Love poetry in comparison to the ballads of Škocjan. Indeed, Postojna, too, has its own murkiness; great depths where the rushing water below can barely be heard, but the eye is able to enjoy crystal miniatures or the largest possible works of art at every step.

100   Carnic Lily (Lilium carniolicum)

101

How the Postojna Caves were gradually revealed

It is already possible to comprehend how the history of Postojna Caves is, in its own way, also a history of the human imagination. To begin with, this fantasy was marked with fear. Man is a creature of the sun and is thus always slightly at the mercy of claustrophobia. Darkness is the concept of evil and danger in every civilisation; in this underworld, daylight is extinguished after only a few tens of metres. So it was that the first deeper penetrations into the cave world were only for the most courageous, for self-control, skill, overcoming natural and civilisation's warnings within oneself. All evil, the devil included, is stored below ground – it is even said that Dante found the inspiration for his Hell

100-102 Outside, various lilies (Lilium martagon, carniolicum, bulbiferum – the martagon, carnic and orange lilies). Below the WHALE'S GUILLET and RUSSIAN PILLARS.

102

103

103   Peony (Paeonia officinalis)

103, 104 Suddenly perceived from the train, the CYPRESS TREES, slim stalagmites in serried rows as similarly soft and mild as the translucent sunlight in the silky flower chalices of the peonies above.

105, 106 Pearly pans and crystalline honeycombs gleam as if from some goldsmith's or jeweller's display.

in "The Divine Comedy" in the Slovene sub-Alpine Karst. With their impermanence and their interweaving of dancing shadows, torches, oil lamps, candles and burning straw trusses only emphasised and invited a diversity of fantastic, even horrific forms. Ordinarily similar to all manner of things, the stone and sinter formations are certainly even stranger in poor and uneven illumination. The first person to record the Postojna Caves, Janez Vajkard Valvasor, also made some drawings at the time – of fossilised animals and people, about which he wrote: "In some places you see terrifying heights, elsewhere everything is in columns so strangely shaped as to seem like some creepy-crawly, snake or other animal in front of one; various terrible forms and grimacing faces and apparitions and the like. The corners, crevices, ground and columns are so full of these that many are filled with horror. The repulsion and fear are even greater because these are also many corridors, hollows, deep chasms and also corridors and fissures up into the heights. In short, a terrifyingly gloomy impression that cannot be described with the pen." Of course, this half-blind, half-frightened stumbling around the infinite labyrinth led to confusion about the sense of distance and of its extent, so that later researchers accused Valvasor of excessiveness and exaggeration of the facts. How could there be two leagues into the interior they said; right up to Čeč's discovery of 1818, it was impossible to enter further than 175 Viennese klafter – some 300 metres into the interior. And the tale of depths, where a stone thrown in would echo only – after reciting two "Our Fathers" was also a tall story. According to Valvasor some chasms were so deep they never returned an echo, or it lost itself in lateral galleries and tunnels.

Valvasor was, anyway, patriotically convinced the Postojna Caves were by far the strangest and most fearful and thus the most interesting and he personally accompanied some English and Dutch acquaintances into them, thereby adding to their fame. During the 18th century, these tales of the fantastic, the pagan or the enchanted gradually developed into a rational curiosity, into a searching for causes and explanations. The first Englishman to describe the Postojna Caves, world traveller Jeremiah Milles, visited the caves in 1736–37 when barely twenty years old, to view the Black Cave, known at that time as the Magdalene Cave, to describe it with a mixture of awe and intelligence: "This is by far the most extraordinary of all we have ever seen and over – reaches the above-mentioned (the known entrance to the caves) in quality and variety of fossils, of which every part of it is so full I cannot even think of describing details of any kind. I must say that for such an interesting site as this cave is, it is visited by very few travellers indeed. Although it is not far from the road, the majority of people travelling along this route are firmly convinced there is nothing worth looking at in Capriola" (land of goats – is this ironic word play on Carniola – the Kranj regions?).

Only a little later, in 1748, the first map of the parts of the cave known at that time came into being, by order of the Habsburg court, devised by the Court mathematician JN Nagel, who also left his signature in the cave itself. His example was soon followed by the famous Breton–Carniolan naturalist, Balthazar Hacquet, the hydrotechnician Tobija Gruber, half-brother to the better known Jesuit, astronomer, technician and generally gifted Gabriel Gruber, who left a legacy of important constructions in Ljubljana and even began the draining of the Ljubljana marshland, known as Barje. There, subterranean waters flow beneath a large, almost 2,000 km² area, to include those from the Postojna Caves. Even as poetic a soul as Johann Gottfried Seume was enthusiastic, but also reasonable in his description of the caves. In his youth, Seume had been sold as a soldier to America by his native lord, and later, towards the end of his short intensive life, was unable to settle down from the travelling, military work, teaching and poetry writing of wich his life consisted. His essay of 1803 "A Walk in Syracuse", is a literary travelogue in the form of letters to a friend about his nine months walk from Leipzig to southern Italy and back. The journal is crammed full of resistance to authority and dictatorships of any kind, but also full of travel descriptiveness. Of Postojna Caves, he wrote: "Beneath us we hear the water, above and around us is the dark night of a broad, high cave. Guides here usually light straw trusses on the rocky walls. The magical illumination of these subterranean sceneries, with natural bridges, fantastic rocky arches, grotesque walls and deep flowing river was one of the most beautiful scenes I can remember. As the straw bundle begins to burn down, they usually throw it from the bridge into the chasm, where it glows in the water channel for a few moments. The sudden extensive illumination and darkness immediately afterwards, into which the feeble light of the torch shines only a few steps ahead, create unexpected contrasts."

Whether revealing new sections and galleries, whether consolidating the easy paths for tourism and business with this natural site of interest, whether investigating the special terrestrial, vital phenomena within, everyone that later thrust into the cave in a pioneering spirit did so systematically and intelligently.

Immediately after 1818, on the occasion of the Emperor's visit, additional lighting was installed and wooden stairways were erected over high walls, allowing 100 people to ascend simultaneously or descend without danger. 1821 saw Ljubljana host the Congress of the Holy Alliance, a month-long meeting of the Russian Tsar, the King of Naples and the representative of the Habsburg Emperor, filling the town with countless high lords. A trip to the caves of Postojna was included in the leisure programme, some ten hours by coach, then on foot into the interior.

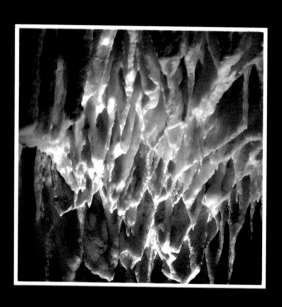

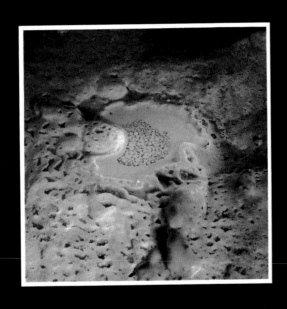

107   The Ravenska Cave

107, 108   A crystalline aragonite hedgehog and the GIANT,
double column of monumental beauty and dimensions.

109 The BRILLIANT is always the centre of wonder and awe.

How Postojna's pride in possessing a site of world interest evolved in practical terms

Year by year the cave became more and more accessible to the general public, with diverse entertainment for everyone held within. Englishman John Russell emphasised them upon his visit in 1822: "Inside one of the most spacious and regular of the caves. The floor is completely smooth. In addition to the stone seats provided by the rock itself, wooden benches have been set in a circle, as have some rough candelabras constructed from a wooden cross nailed horizontally to the top of an upright stake. Once a year, on the festival of their patron saint, the farming community of Postojna and its surroundings gather here in this cave to celebrate. Here, several hundred feet away from the earth's surface and a mile from daylight, unpolished Carniolan music echoes through a hall grander than any ever constructed for any ruler. The flames of the lamps reflect from the stalactite walls like the glow of a constantly altering light, and amidst the dancing brightness the village seducers and their beauties twirl and waltz."

Postojna's pride in possessing something of such world interest began to complement itself with practical steps and plans. The first guides, of whom only one knew any other language than Slovene, barely covered the expenses of candle and oil lamp illumination with the "guide tax" charged. For wealthier guests, candles were cut into pieces, one or two guides walking on ahead to set them up and light them. Thus, the traveller arrived with his guide in an already illuminated cave and the shorter candles prevented too long a visit. On occasion, four men with burning torches would walk eight paces in front of the visitors. From 1825 onwards, on Whit Monday, generally considered to be the Postojna Cave Festival day for more than a century, the caves began to be ever increasingly illuminated. To begin with, there were 10 cave lights, 103 oil lamps and 11 candelabras. Attempts were even made to use Bengal lights, but there was too much smoke and they were forbidden. Later, paraffin lamps and magnesium lights like those used in photography were introduced but, by 1884, the first electric light was installed in the cave, arousing a wave of enthusiasm and fresh interest. Technically this illumination was extremely simple: 12 arc lamps on direct current produced at the entrance to the cave with a traction engine housed in a temporary shed. But each arc lamp was as powerful as 1400 candles, and for especially important guests up to an additional 16,000 (!) wax tapers and some 100 oil lamps were lit.

110, 111 A veritable throng of fantastic miniatures, tiny pools, amidst which crouches the sinter form of a stooped DWARF. Candlelight or burning torchlight animate all these forms, arousing man's imagination. Even the first person to give a written description of the Caves, Baron Janez Vajkard Valvasor, spoke of these forms as a collection of turned-to-stone, distorted faces, like some petrified hell, though he also called it "the loveliest and most charming cave" with a "subterranean art collection" (1689)

By 1901 electrical illumination had been modernised using alternating current, and lightbulbs in addition to the arc lamps (36 arc lamps of 2000 watts, almost 1000 lightbulbs). The installations were now partly underground. Further renovations were made in 1928, by which time the network of cables had grown to 30 km and had to be well insulated. All the main cables were laid in wooden ducts and bitumen poured in, the whole then being buried underground or built into the walls. In carrying out this work, the people of Postojna demonstrated infinite ingenuity – even the visitor looking for it will hardly be able to detect a trace of excavation work anywhere. After the Second World War, a high voltage cable was installed in the interior of the caves and a transformer concealed in the Concert Hall. Classical lightbulbs gave way to halogen bulbs, the switching on and off of lights was left to electronics. a diesel generator was prepared should there be a failure in the electricity network.

112

113

112-114 The caves are possibly more magnificent when light only momentarily flashes over them, but the eye cannot find any final corner to reveal them in their entirety. The cave guides nearly always extinguish the lights for a moment or two, for a cold shudder to run through the visitors, so unused to such total darkness. Since 1884, electricity has permitted us to satisfy our curiosity, perceiving nearly everything. Initially the cables were laid in hollowed logs filled with bitumen. Cables today have been hidden even more skilfully and the majority of lights are not visible other than where their contribution is required, such as the candelabra in the DANCE HALL. One or two of the oldest lanterns have been preserved as museum pieces.

Such consistent illumination has perhaps caused the gigantic underground spaces to lose some of their mystery, since everything, right to the last corner, is visible. Only here and there does the darkness reach into the depths, permitting a sense of unknown dangers. On the other hand, progressive lighting has brought closer such diverse beauty and points of interest that the eye would not otherwise detect, and has rendered the caves extremely pleasant, which more than compensates for the loss.

116

115, 116 The path from the BRILLIANT leads for some way through the SNOWY HALL, its white sinter roof truly reminiscent of a winter's fairytale. In the half kilometre long SMALL GALLERIES (a section of the galleries not usually on general view), the dripstone formations are particularly abundant. The mighty GOTHIC PILLAR supports two sloping ceilings with extraordinarily effective natural architecture.

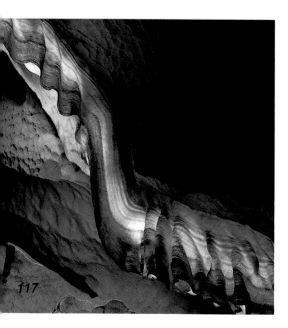

117

For a long while, one's feet also suffered, for the caves could only be entered on foot and the paths were littered with stones and other obstacles. In 1857, sedan chairs of varying degrees of comfort were introduced for those of greater means and 1872 saw the first tracks laid for two-seater carriages, though this was not a cheap form of transport. From 1914 onwards, small petrol locomotives pulled trains though the cave, with as many as 150 people a once. However, exhaust fumes created too many problems in the caves, filling them with haze and strong fumes and, in 1959, the petrol engines were replaced by electric ones. A circular track of 3,750 metres was constructed in 1968, thereby increasing the transport capacity and allowing some 15,000 people a day to visit the caves. Nowadays, the tourist only walks about one and a half kilometres on foot in the most interesting and picturesque sections.

Needless to say, all this development was accompanied by an increase in literature of every sort, particularly tourist guide books. Some years ago, the speleologist and promoter of the caves, Dr. Habe, counted some 90 tourist publications; nowadays there are over 100, of every shape and size, extent and purpose. These range from the first classical edition by Hohenwart, dating from 1830-32 with 19 exclusive pictures, to the latest, most modern editions that include a facsimile edition of Hohenwart. Most of this literature originated spontaneously from professional interest or the care that the administration of Postojna Caves has continuously shown for more than 180 years. A very high percentage of the profits has been re-invested. In 1884, tourist posters in major world languages were sent to spas and railway centres, and to hotels in all the larger towns in Austria, England, France, Germany and Italy. That same year, the Whit Monday train took 6,000 visitors into Postojna Caves! Illuminated information panels were set up throughout Europe, with depictions of stalactites and other curiosities. The area rapidly became one of the greatest tourist attractions of the Austro-Hungarian empire. In 1894, tourist traffic here was almost equal that of Lake Garda and in excess of that of Badgastein, Bad Aussee or Villach. Even Bled attracted only one seventh of that number of visitors the same year.

Gradually a visit to the Postojna Caves became a matter of prestige. After the first enthusiastic royal "natural scientists", a succession of members of the imperial Habsburg line arrived here. After Franz I came the Crown Price Ferdinand, Maria Louisa, Franz Joseph I with his wife Elizabeth, Crown Prince Karel and so on, followed by the kings of Saxony, Greece, Serbia, Romania, Sweden,Norway, Italy, Denmark – and, usually, all the queens; the Brazilian and Ethiopian Emperors, a Japanese prince, a princess of China and a long line of state presidents and ministers including Krushchev and Brezhnev, plus a variety of famous artists and scientists. A welcome guest who visited the caves several times was Marshal Tito. Eventually it was neither a matter of prestige nor of protocol – visitors simply turned into the millions whose contemporary curiosity or enjoyment of nature or love of beauty brings them here year after year.

117, 118 Almost incredibly, dreamy LACE looped from the ceiling. And countless filigree motifs in pastel and watercolours. As we wander through the caves we ponder whether the human hand would be capable of such work, even given a hundred thousand years and great talent. Upon entering Postojna, one of the world's greatest contemporary sculptors, Henry Moore, uttered words to the effect that this was Mother Nature's greatest art gallery!

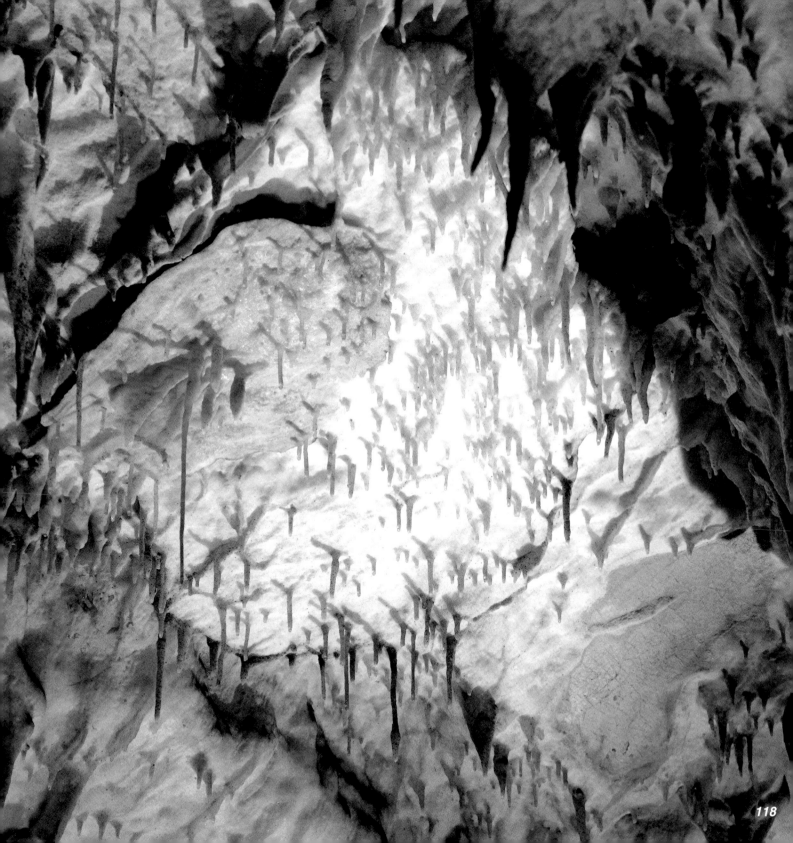

119

An intermingling of nature and culture in Postojna's marvel

119, 120 The gigantic CONCERT HALL (3,000 m³) has sufficient space for 10,000 people. Musicians as famous as Enrico Caruso have performed here. Symphony orchestras, the world renowned Slovene Octet and a variety of soloists appear here. The acoustics here are exceptional, although almost impossible for sound-recording. Visible and invisible spaces return so many echoes in so many ways as to render the music mystical and truly tumultuous, though lingering secretively to the sensitive ear. Without exaggeration, a concert in this hall is a unique experience.

Briefly stated, the events connected with Postojna's wonders over the past 180+ years have been the blossoming of a particularly special culture. Ancient romantics defined culture as everything man creates apart from nature. Here in Postojna, culture and nature are intertwined in a most beautiful and extraordinarily interesting whole. Not merely a matter of technical prowess, natural science or tourist culture, this is a total interaction of human and natural creativity. With its darkness and gloom, extraordinary forms and sounds, the cave has been since its primordial beginnings a kind of mirror of human existence causing visitors to acknowledge with much sentiment that which they bear within themselves. Even Hohenwart and his contemporaries perceived in the caves The Union of Two Hearts; St. Peter's Throne; the Mummies and the Bell; the Cypress, the Curtain; the Red Sea; Calvary; the Cappucian and the Dripping Fountain. Later poetry (rather than just a need for directions) added to and altered these names decade after decade: the Capsized Boat; Snow Mountain; Canopy; Congress Hall (host to the 1965 World Speleological Congress); the Tortoise; the Corn Cob (a three metre stalactite); the five metre high Cone; the Laundry; the Female Breast; the Pans; the Tent; Charcoal Kilns; Lace; the Sunflower; the Turkish Pipe; the Gnome; the Alley of Columns; Father Christmas; the 16 metre high stalagmite Skyscraper; the Magical Garden; the Cockerel; the Parrot; the Russian Bridge; the Brilliant; the Tower of Pisa; Macaroni; the Red and White Hall; Moses, the Madonna and Child; Muslim cemetery, the Tiger, the Lions and the Owl and the Winter and Concert halls. Every tourist can view it all for himself and further secluded sections contain even more wonders. There is hardly an object or concept that the human eye has not perceived fossilised here, like Snow White before the arrival of the Prince who kissed away the spell. Every traveller to Postojna Caves wonders and marvels for him or herself, thereby adding one's own fragment to its mighty cultural image; patiently, person by person, thought by thought like the water with its millennia of dripping, building its subterranean fantasies. In closer detail, like the waters united in the created drop, the Slovene poet Oton Župančič wrote:

> Embryo waters: the Karst rocks cradle
> Invisible seeds of rivers, lakes: fusing
> Atoms in millions, one single forming
> Drop shaping into pure oval.
> We would say: the invisible seeds of a subterranean wonder – made celestial through the heart of man.

121

121–123 Hanging above is the FADED CURTAIN, to the right the
PANCETA – cured bacon as it is dried in layers in local homes.
On the far right is the CAULIFLOWER.

122

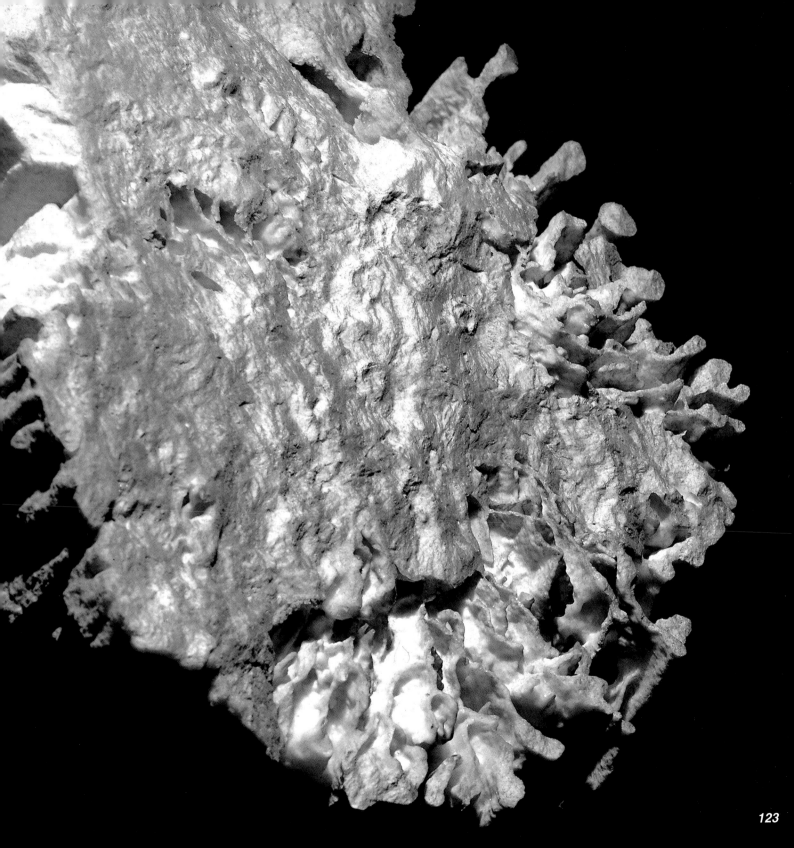

124

124-126 A stony CRESTED HEN perches on a rock. Millimetre thin curtains again hang from the ceiling, sometimes tattered at the edges, sometimes artistically heavy brocade, such as the GREAT CURTAIN in green, grey and brown.

127-134 The entrance into the BEAUTIFUL CAVE is like some vast cathedral. An infinite and immense calm emanates from this cave, where magnificent asceticism and almost dissolute beauty unite. Once again, on the following page, lace and columns alternate, thousands of tiny stalactites on the ceiling, white-as-snow pearls from the floor. From time to time, the water flowing down can be observed, though with difficulty, for it is so pure and clear. The BRILLIANT with its admirers again, and then its peak, with the rainbow hues of a true diamond. Further on, some more views of the BEAUTIFUL CAVE, like it's an other world.

125

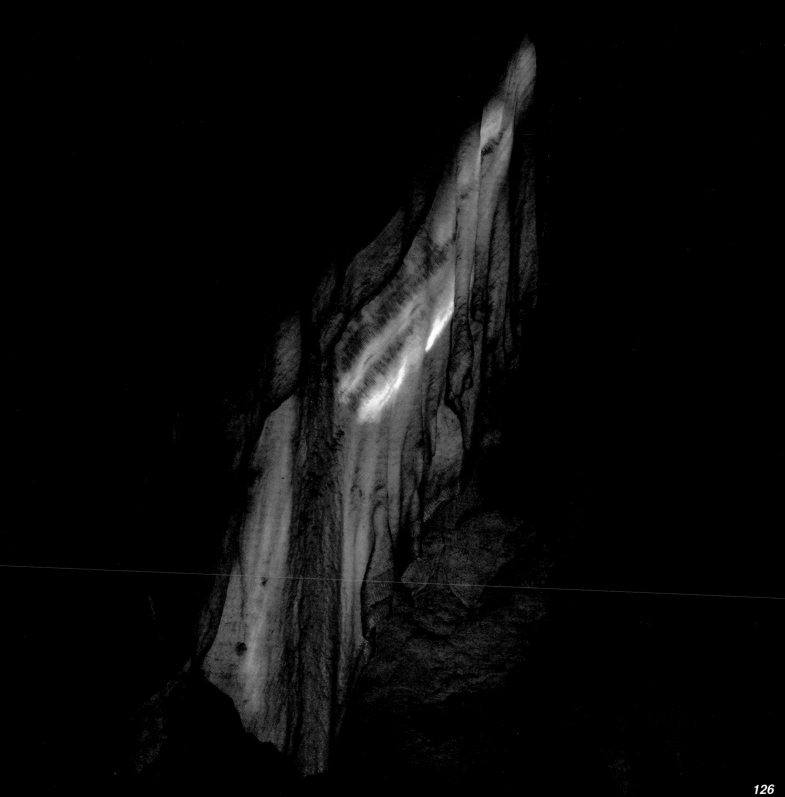

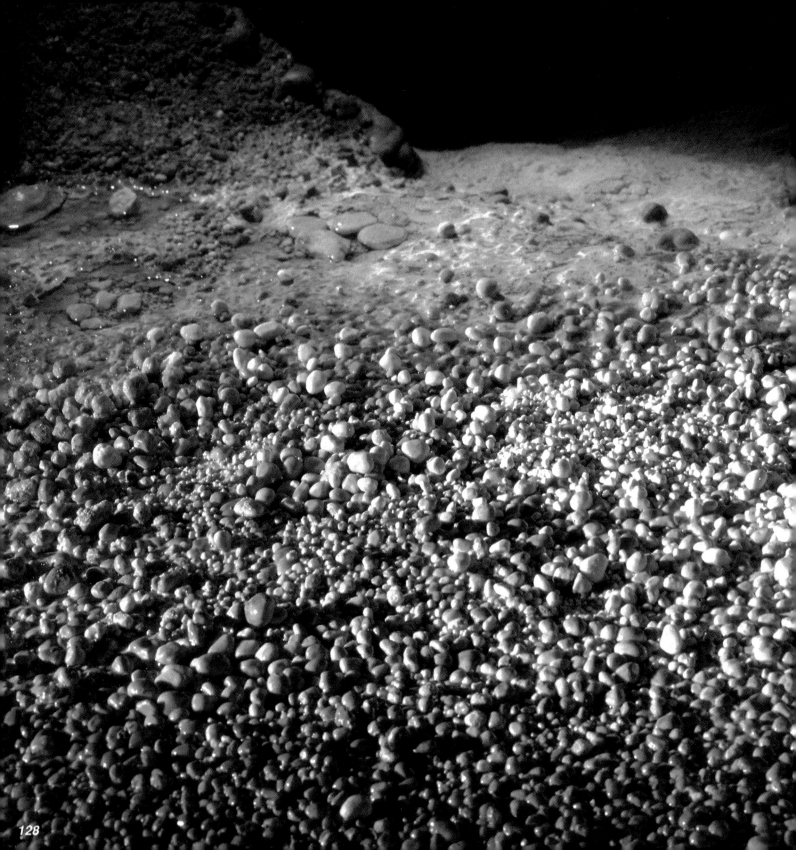

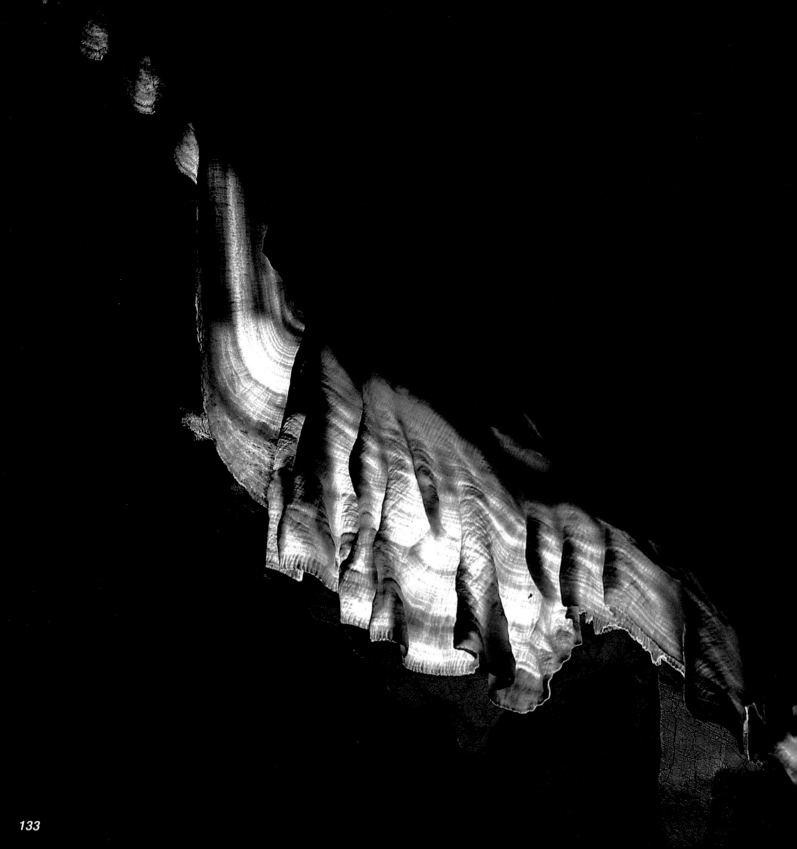

135

135 - 137 At the pathside squats another stone bird - the PARROT. The small train, not running as fast as might be deduced from the picture, rushes beneath the gigantic COLLAPSED PILLAR, a kind of Ionic work of art. Large old candelabras hang from the roof, a souvenir of the past.

Today, when awareness of the responsibility for all that nature has given us and that our predecessors preserved and handed down to us is becoming a significant part of our modern world, it is worth remembering that the first administrators of Postojna Caves, over 180 years ago, were fully aware of the danger of destruction of the frail, crystalline structures in the underworld. Even then, vandalism was cautioned against and effective supervision of visitors imposed. Later construction of paths, lighting and other necessary additions were exemplary in this aspect. Contemporary problems of ecologically safeguarding the caves are more sensitive: mass visits bring microclimatic changes into the interior; illumination during the season for almost the entire length of the day is altering conditions for the cave fauna, and producing layers of algae on the stalagmites and stalactites, just as the soot from oil lamps and torches did in the past. The relative humidity, and with it the microflora, is altering; rapid rotting of wood and corrosion of iron in structures demands a search for newer, more durable materials. Various industrial and sewage pollution flows into the underworld with the running waters. All this is an important part of caring for the caves today, carried out not only by the administration but also by various institutions, including the Karst Research Institute of the Slovene Academy of Sciences and Arts, located in Postojna itself.

As the tourist steps through the gate over which "Immensum ad antrum aditus" is written and, a little disturbed, is led inwards, he or she should understand that, for two short hours, noisy daily life will be left behind in exchange for a silent, yet extremely eloquent history – both terrestrial and human. Time immemorial, infinite earthly energy and patience, and an equal amount of human will, expectation and creativity is to be found in these wonderful forms, spaces, stone, crystals, quietness and rushing. The first great space, once the entrance or even the main cave used to be known as the Cathedral a reminder of the kind of solemnity that overcomes man as he steps from one world into another. From the world of the sun into Tartarus, from the world of reality into a world of marvels and sublime uncertainty.

Immensum ad antrum aditus.

138   The intermittent Cerknica Lake
       (Cerkniško jezero)

139   Bloke Lake (Bloško jezero)

140   Sumac (Rhus cotinus)

138, 139 After the final return from the underground, after the stony, dark drama, the traveller gladly rests by sunny, sheltered idylls such as the Cerknica lake or the Lily Lake at Bloke. Countless subterranean images fill one's mind, as do the ballads to the incomprehensibility of this world. Perhaps, at least a little, one feels like the mythical god, Triglav, one of whose three heads used to peer into the underworld.

140 In the autumn, Cotinus colours this dry, drained, sunny, stony and yet overgrown region with such a surprising red that words to describe it are hard to find.